A New True Book

UNDERGROUND LIFE

By Allan Roberts

This "true book" was prepared
under the direction of
Illa Podendorf,
formerly with the Laboratory School,
University of Chicago

Ⴔ CHILDRENS PRESS, CHICAGO

Bull snake gliding into
a prairie dog's burrow

PHOTO CREDITS

Lynn M. Stone—2, 4 (2 photos, bottom), 23 (top left), 24, 28 (2 photos, middle and bottom)

Allan Roberts—4 (top left), 7, 8, 9, 10 (2 photos), 15, 17 (2 photos), 18, 19 (2 photos), 20 (right), 21 (right), 23 (top and bottom right), 26 (2 photos), 27, 31 (2 photos), 32 (2 photos), 33, 35, 37, 43 (left), 45 (5 photos)

Jerry Hennen—4 (top right), 20 (left), 41, 43 (right), 45 (top right)

Reinhard Brucker—cover, 23 (bottom left)

James P. Rowan—12, 14, 16 (2 photos), 21 (left), 38 (left), 45 (bottom left)

Tony Freeman—13, 28 (top)

Chris Hagel—38 (right)

Cover: Badger at entrance to its underground home

U. 83 Pub 5.95

Library of Congress Cataloging in Publication Data

Roberts, Allan.
  Underground life.

  (A New true book)
  Includes index.
  Summary: Describes the characteristics and habits of a variety of insects and animals that live in the soil or in caves.
  1. Soil fauna—Juvenile literature. 2. Cave fauna—Juvenile literature. [1. Soil animals.
2. Cave animals] I. Title.
QL110.R6 1983   591.909'48   82-23582
ISBN 0-516-01689-X   AACR2

TABLE OF CONTENTS

Above left: Adult mole cricket lives underground and eats roots.
Above right: Golden mantled ground squirrel
Below: Gopher tortoise (left) and its underground burrow (right)

WHY DO ANIMALS LIVE UNDERGROUND?

Life under your feet?
Yes, there are many living
things found under the
ground.

Many animals live under
the ground. It is cooler
during the hot weather. It
is warmer in cold weather.
It is also safer. Many
animals hide from their
enemies underground.

HUMANS UNDERGROUND

Today some people work underground. Coal and diamonds are dug up underground. Wine and cheese are made in some caves.

Sod houses were cooler in summer and warmer in winter.

Many pioneers lived
partly under the ground in
"sod" houses on the
prairie. These houses even
had dirt and grass on their
roofs!

Cave used by Arizona Indians seven hundred years ago. Now it is a preserved cliff dwelling at Tonto National Monument.

Many early Indians lived in caves. Their old tools have been found in caves. Today some humans build their homes and barns underground!

Can you see the roots of
this young walnut tree?

UNDERGROUND
ROOTS

Green plants must have
sunlight to make sugar for
food. These plants can
only have their roots
underground. Their roots
give support and bring in
water.

The giant sequoia tree grows from a seed the size of your fingernail.

Green plants make seeds. Seeds have food in them. This food is used for the baby plant to start growing. Many kinds of seeds live in the ground.

Some seeds can live underground for fifty or more years before growing.

Most of the food we eat comes from seeds. We eat the seeds of corn, wheat, rice, and barley. We make breads and other foods from these seeds.

Have you ever eaten a peanut, onion, radish, beet, or turnip? All of these foods are roots that grow underground.

The common morel is a fungus.

UNDERGROUND PLANTS AND ANIMALS

Fungi and bacteria live from the dead materials in the soil.

Most bacteria and fungi cannot be seen with just

your eyes. You must use a
microscope to see them.

Some plants make tiny
spores instead of seeds.
With a microscope you
can see these spores of
bacteria, mushrooms, moss,
and ferns.

Thousands of animals can only be seen with a microscope. Baby spiders, mites, springtails, and insects all live underground.

Earthworms live underground. They help to make good soil. With good soil our plants will grow.

Earthworm

Cross section of underground ant colony showing tunnels with cocoons

Ants live underground. A queen ant lays the eggs. Worker ants build the tunnels, look for food, and feed the young. Some ants even have soldiers to guard the nest.

Above: North American
termites
Right: Giant African
termite nest

In North America, the
termite nest is in the
ground. Workers go to the
surface to find wood to
eat.

In Africa, termites build
big nests above the ground.

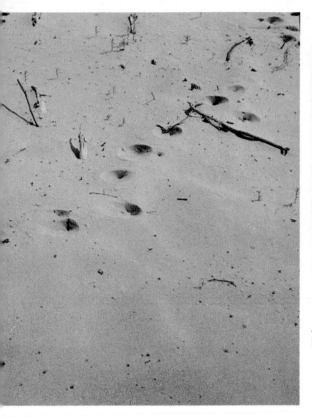

Above: Newly hatched ant lion
Left: Traps made by ant lions in
the sand

The ant lion makes holes in the ground and waits at the bottom of these holes. When an ant falls in this "trap" it is quickly caught and eaten.

17

Seventeen-year cicadas with shedded skins

There is one insect that spends seventeen years underground! During the last year of its life it comes to the surface. It then sheds its skin and turns into what we call the seventeen-year cicada.

A mole's fur will lay smooth and flat going either forward or backward. This is so moles can move quickly in either direction in their tunnels.

UNDERGROUND MAMMALS

Moles very seldom come above ground. They eat insects and worms in the ground.

19

Above: Shrews are the only North American mammals that have a poison. Their poison is mild, but it can kill mice and insects.
Right: Close-up of a red fox

Shrews spend most of their time underground. Red foxes also dig homes in the ground.

UNDERGROUND MOUNTAIN ANIMALS

Two animals, the pika and marmot, live in cracks in rocks. They use their tunnels all year.

The pika stores grass at the bottom of its burrow. The pika will eat this grass during the winter.

Both the yellowbelly marmots (left) and the pika (right) use "alarm whistles" when they see an enemy.

LIFE IN THE DESERT AND PRAIRIE

Both these areas get very hot. Also there are not many places to hide from enemies.

Many animals have solved both of these problems. Rats, mice, and armadillos all spend the daytime in their burrows. Here it is both safe and cool.

Armadillos (above left),
kangaroo rats (above right), young
coyotes, or pups, (left), and
badgers spend the daylight hours
in their burrows.

Badgers and coyotes
also sleep much of the
day in their underground
homes. When it is cooler,
they come out to find food.

Prairie dogs

Prairie dogs eat plants during the day. But they do not wander far from their burrows.

LIFE AROUND LAKES, PONDS, AND STREAMS

There are millions of insects and worms that live underground along wet areas. This is why so many birds hunt for food in these areas. One group of such birds is called the "shorebirds."

Both the woodcock (above) and the crayfish (right) hunt in wetlands.

The woodcock has an extra long and very sensitive beak. The beak is used for sticking into the mud to catch worms.

The crayfish makes holes around the water's edge. At night it comes out to eat.

The muskrat and beaver make large mud-and-stick homes in the water. The entrances are below the water's surface. By having such homes they are safe from foxes and coyotes.

A mud-and-stick beaver house is called a lodge.

Top: The ocean at low tide
Middle left: Steamer clams
Middle right: Atlantic blue
crab
Right: Ghost crab digging its
burrow.

28

LIFE ALONG THE SEASHORE

Ocean water along the shores and beaches moves up and down at different times of the day. Such movements are called "tides."

Millions of animals live along such shores. Worms, clams, insects, and crabs have learned to make tunnels in such areas.

UNDERGROUND EGGS

If you were a baby grasshopper, cricket, or tumblebug, you would be born in darkness! All these insects lay eggs under the ground.

The tumblebug is most interesting. The parents find some rotting animal waste (manure) and roll it up into a ball. Their eggs

Tumblebugs at work. These insects clean up the earth. In Texas, 80 percent of the cattle droppings are sometimes removed by these insects.

are put inside the ball. Then the ball is buried in the ground. The young hatch and feed upon the animal waste!

Digger wasps (right) and some snakes, such as the rough green snake (above), lay thèir eggs in the ground.

Many wasps dig tunnels in the ground. At the end of these tunnels they place a "stung" insect or spider. The wasp then lays an egg upon the paralyzed animal. The tunnel is closed with dirt. When the young hatch, they eat the victim.

Scientists even have found fossilized dinosaur eggs. These eggs were laid underground millions of years ago!

Some birds dig tunnels and lay their eggs inside.

In the Arctic there are many birds that raise their young in tunnels.

Bank swallows lay their eggs and raise their young inside tunnels.

HIBERNATING UNDERGROUND

Many animals hibernate during the cold winter months. During this sleep, the heartbeat drops and the body chemistry slows down. These animals live off stored body fat.

Some bears, mice, chipmunks, ground squirrels, and groundhogs sleep underground.

Close-up of the winter nest of a hibernating meadow mouse.

Snakes will sometimes use these same holes. Since snakes are not warm-blooded, the holes must be deep. If not deep, their blood would freeze and kill them.

WHAT IS A CAVE ?

Natural caves are formed in areas where the rock can be eroded and dissolved by water.

Underground caves are different sizes. Some are very small. Others have miles and miles of caverns!

Clear pool inside Carlsbad Caverns

Some caves are dry. Streams and even small lakes are inside some caves!

Scientists have discovered an entire ancient Indian camp inside a cave.

Some Indians built "cliff dwellings." Small cities were built inside a single natural cave!

Cliff-dwellings at Mesa Verde National Park (above) and Montezuma Castle National Monument (right) tell us much about Indian life hundreds of years ago.

Caves in other parts of the world also have been used by ancient humans. In Europe cave paintings of animals were made upon the walls. Some of these animals are now extinct!

Entire skeletons of other ancient animals also have been uncovered inside caves.

LIFE IN CAVES

Many animals use only the entrance of a cave. This is because beyond the entrance, the cave is completely dark.

Raccoons, foxes, rats, mice, and other mammals will live near the entrance. Hawks, owls, wrens, swallows, and other birds will also use the front part of a cave.

Close-up of an Indiana bat

Deep inside the cave,
animals need special
methods of surviving. Bats
can live here.

Most bats are insect-
eating mammals. They
hang inside the cool cave
during the day. In the

evening, they fly out of the cave in search of food.

Bats are not blind. However, inside a deep cave there is no light. Therefore, bats use sound to fly in the dark. Each bat sends out sounds that bounce off the cave walls. The bats hear the echo of the noise. By using these sounds, bats can fly safely around inside caves.

Above: Mexican freetail bats
leaving their cave
Left: Close-up of hibernating
brown bats.

Some bats fly hundreds or thousands of miles to hibernate in caves. During this winter sleep, bats live off stored fat. In the spring, they fly back to their summer homes.

Flies, cave crickets, millipedes, cave spiders and some salamanders live in caves, too.

In the streams and lakes of caves, isopods can be seen in the water. Some caves even have the blind cave fish.

Another blind cave animal is the crayfish. It is not a fish at all. The blind crayfish is related to the shrimp, lobsters, and crabs of the ocean.

Top left: Indiana blind cave fish
Top middle: Close-up of a cave spider
Top right: Cave cricket
Middle left: Blind cave crayfish
Middle: Cave isopod in stream
Middle right: Cave salamander
Left: Millipedes

As you have seen, the ground is full of living things. Each one is important to our world.

WORDS YOU SHOULD KNOW

ancient(AIN • chent) — very old; of times long ago

bacteria(back • TEER • eeya) — tiny organisms that can be seen only with a microscope

burrows(BER • rohs) — to dig into the ground and make a hole or tunnel

dissolve(dih • ZOLVE) — to mix a solid into a liquid

enemy(EN • ih • me) — not a friend

erode(E • road) — to wear away bit by bit

extinct(x • TINKT) — no longer around; not in existance

fossilize(FAWSS • ill • ize) — to become a fossil

fungi(FUNG • eye) — a group of organisms that have no flowers, leaves, or green coloring; mushrooms, molds, and yeast

hibernate(HI • ber • nait) — to spend the winter asleep in a protected place

microscope(MIKE • roh • skohpe) — an instrument that makes very small things look larger

sensitive(SEN • sih • tiv) — able to react to light, sound, smell, touch, or taste easily

sequoia(sih • KWOI • ah) — a very large evergreen tree

sod(SAHD) — a piece of grass and soil held together by matted roots

spore(SPOR) — a tiny part of certain organisms that have no flowers

tide(TYDE) — the regular change in the level of oceans and other large bodies of water caused by the pull of the moon and the sun on the earth

INDEX

About the Author

*Allan Roberts received his undergraduate degree from Earlham
College. As a participant in the National Science Foundation
Academic Year Institute, he received his master's degree from the
University of Georgia. Currently a biology teacher at Richmond
High School in Richmond, Indiana, Allan has taught for more than
twenty-three years. In addition to his regular classroom activities,
he has taught at Indiana Extension University and special classes
for the young. Many of his research articles and photographs have
been published. His photographs also have appeared in the*
National Geographic, Reader's Digest, Audubon, National Wildlife,
and many textbooks.